LOSE WEIGHT

The best healthy recipes for your Thermomix

By Laura Taylor

Table of Contents

1. Introduction 1

2. Soups 2

   2.1 Melon and cucumber soup 2

   2.2 Vegetables Soup 3

   2.3 Cabbage soup 5

   2.4 Sauerkraut soup 7

   2.5 Parsnip soup 8

   2.6 Red cabbage soup 10

   2.7 Broccoli soup with curry 12

   2.8 Cauliflower soup with cream cheese 14

   2.9 Mint soup 15

   2.10 Sweet potato soup 16

3. Salads 17

   3.1 Carrot salad 17

   3.2 Apple and dates salad 18

   3.3 Pepper salad 19

   3.4 Kohlrabi sald 21

   3.5 Broccoli salad 22

   3.6 White cabbage salad 23

   3.7 Carrot and apple salad 25

   3.8 Raw salad 26

   3.9 Bean salad 27

3.10 Papaya salad 29

4. Main courses 31

4.1 Potato and cauliflower stew 31

4.2 Tomato and arugula risotto 33

4.3 Beans stew 35

4.4 Chicken, vegetables and rice stew 37

4.5 Curry and vegetables rice 39

4.6 Vegetable stuffed peppers 41

4.7 Squids... 43

4.8 Noodles wth salmon 45

4.9 Salmon fillet with potatoes and broccoli 47

4.10 Cauliflower and zucchini pancakes.................... 49

5. Desserts 50

5.1 Pear mousse with chia seeds 50

5.2 Fruit ice cream 51

5.3 Banana ice cream with basil.................................. 52

5.4 Ginger tea 53

5.5 Strawberry milkshake.. 54

5.6 Yogurt ice cream with strawberry sauce 55

5.7 Lemon tea with ginger... 57

5.8 Orange and pineapple smoothie............................ 58

5.9 Raspberry ice cream.. 59

5.10 Fruit salad with raspberry yogurt 60

6. Appetizers, dipping sauces and spreads 62

6.1 Tomato and cottage cheese dipping sauce 62

6.2 Spreading avocado and dates cream 63

6.3 Spreading salmon cream 64

6.4 Dates dipping sauce 65

6.5 Persimmon jam 66

6.6 Eggplant pesto 67

6.7 Yogurt appetizer with fruit and muesli 69

6.8 Spreading bean cream 71

6.9 Dates and sesame spreading cream 72

6.10 Turkish style spreading cream 73

1. INTRODUCTION

The following selection of recipes will go a long way to help you lose weight, and it does so in multiple ways:

1) **Quick and easy preparation using the Thermomix**

   - The Thermomix assists you with the tedious work of cutting the vegetables
   - Saving the cumulative amount of time spent in the preparation process
   - Making healthy food in the face of limited time is made possible as the device gets the work done really fast and healthily

1) **Low calorie dishes**

   - Renouncing fats as much as possible, especially foods containing fatty acids such as butter or cream, etc.
   - Also, renouncing sugar as much as possible. Instead, we will use foods with complex carbohydrates as well as rice that despite their low calories offer a long feeling of satiety

2) **See: Different ways of cooking**

   - This recipe book allows you to create menus with up to 5 plates, as it gives directions for making soups, salads, main courses, sweets and desserts. In addition to appetizers and sauces

2. SOUPS

2.1 Melon and cucumber soup

INGREDIENTS

4 PORTIONS

- 1 Melon
- 1 salad cucumber
- 150g of Chicken bouillon cubes
- 100g of Cream Cheese: cucumber-garlic-dill flavored
- Salt
- White pepper

PREPARATION

- Cut the melon in 4 parts
- Set a part of the melon aside to decorate later
- Remove the seeds and skin the melon properly
- Peel the cucumber and cut lengthwise, afterwards remove the seeds with a spoon
- Cut melon and cucumber into dice shapes
- Mix all the ingredients, including bouillon cube and cheese, in the mixing bowl
- Puree for 30 Seconds / Speed 8
- Add salt and pepper to taste and let it cool
- From the saved melon, use a melon baller/parisienne scoop to add a ball to the soup as decoration

2.2 Vegetables Soup

INGREDIENTS

4 PORTIONS

- 1 onion
- 1 garlic clove
- 1 teaspoon of red curry paste
- 10g coconut oil
- 750g of Water
- 1-2 tablespoons vegetable broth
- 1 teaspoon of salt
- 1 pinch of pepper
- 250g of mixed cooked vegetables
- (Egg rolled mushrooms, zucchini, peppers, broccoli florets, fennel, onions or peas)
- 80g of cream cheese with herbs
- ½ banana
- 1 teaspoon of blueberries

PREPARATION

- Cut the onion and garlic clove, then chop for 5 seconds / Speed 5
- Add the curry paste and coconut oil, let it stew for 2 minutes / Varoma / Speed 1
- Add the vegetables, cut into large pieces 7 seconds / Speed 6

3

- Accumulate water, chicken broth, salt and pepper at the base of Varoma
- Quickly add vegetables, and cook for 15 minutes / Varoma / Speed 1
- Add fresh cheese, medium banana and puree for 30 seconds / Speed 10

2.3 Cabbage soup

INGREDIENTS

4 PORTIONS

- 500g white cabbage in large pieces
- 1 chopped pepper
- 50g of onions
- 500g of water
- 1 vegetable broth cube
- 150g of celery cut into slices ½ cm
- 150g of sliced carrots
- 150g of leek in rings
- 1 tablespoon of soy sauce
- ¼ teaspoon of black pepper
- ½ teaspoon of salt
- ¼ teaspoon of liquid sweetener
- 1 teaspoon of rapeseed oil
- 1 can of tomato sauce 400g

PREPARATION

- Add the cabbage, pepper and onion to the mixing bowl.
- Let it cut for 8 seconds / Speed 5, hasten it with the spatula
- Add all ingredients except the tomato sauce
- Let it cook for 20 Minutes / 100 ° C / Counterclockwise / Speed 2

- Add the tomato sauce and let it cook 5 minutes more / Counterclockwise / Speed 2

2.4 Sauerkraut soup

INGREDIENTS

4 PORTIONS

- 1 piece of pepper, small pieces or strips
- 1-2 balls of onions
- Garlic Clove
- 1 sliced carrot
- 1 canned mushrooms
- ½ small can of crushed tomatoes
- 1chicken bouillon cube
- Salt, pepper and paprika to taste
- Pack of lean ham in dice
- 300g of sauerkraut

PREPARATION

- Add the onion and garlic, cook for about 7 Seconds / Power 8
- Sauté together with the diced ham and a little bit of oil for 5 minutes / Varoma / Speed 2
- Add the remaining ingredients
- Add approximately 600 ml of water, so that all the ingredients are covered with water
- Cook it for 25 Minutes / 100 ° C / Speed 2 in the opposite direction /counterclockwise

2.5 Parsnip soup

INGREDIENTS

4 PORTIONS

- 300g of onions
- Garlic cloves
- 20g of olive oil
- 50g of potatoes, weighed after peeled
- 350g of parsnip, weighed after peeled
- 750g of water
- 1 teaspoon seasoning powder or a chicken bouillon cube
- 1 teaspoon of curry
- ½ teaspoon of dill
- 12g of cooking cream
- ½ teaspoon of pepper
- 1 teaspoon of salt

PREPARATION

- Peel the onions and cut them in halves
- Peel the garlic and add it and the onions to the mixing bowl
- Slice 5 seconds / Power 6, push them down with the spatula
- Add olive oil
- Cooking for 3 minutes in the Varoma / Speed 1

- Peel and cut the parsnip and potatoes into large pieces
- Introduce them into mixing bowl
- Chop for 6 seconds / Speed 6
- Add water, seasoning powder, curry and dill
- Cook for 20 minutes in Varoma / Power 1
- Puree for 20 seconds / Power 7
- Add salt and pepper to the soup, to taste

2.6 Red cabbage soup

INGREDIENTS

4 PORTIONS

- 400g of Red cabbage
- 40g of Shallots
- 40g of butter
- 40g of apples
- 40g of brown Sugar
- ½ teaspoon ground cinnamon
- 25 ml of red wine
- 50g de Blueberries
- 60ml of orange juice
- 800ml of Vegetable Broth
- 200ml of Soy cream
- salt and pepper

PREPARATION

- Chop the shallots
- Press Down 30 Seconds / Speed 5
- Cut the red cabbage with the knife into large pieces
- Remove the seeds of the apples and peel
- Add the red cabbage and apples to the mixing bowl
- Press down 1 minute / Speed 5
- Add the butter
- Cook for 4 minutes / Varoma / Speed 3

- Add sugar and caramelize it, 4 minutes / Varoma / Speed 3
- Spread with red wine and orange juice
- Simmer for 7 minutes / Varoma / Speed 3
- Once you have reduced about 2/3 parts add the vegetable broth and boil
- Add remaining ingredients
- Cooking 20 minutes at 80º C / Varoma / Speed 3
- Finally, blend the soup for 3 minutes / potency 10
- Go through a strainer
- Add salt and pepper to taste

2.7 Broccoli soup with curry

INGREDIENTS

4 PORTIONS

- 1 Garlic clove
- 5g of ginger
- 15g of oil
- 500g of broccoli
- 150g of carrots
- 3 teaspoons of spicy curry
- 600g of water
- 400g of coconut milk
- 2 teaspoons of powder seasoning
- salt and pepper

PREPARATION

- Introduce the garlic clove and the ginger into the mixing bowl
- Chop for 5 seconds / Speed 5
- Add the 15g of oil
- Cook for 2 minutes / Varoma / Speed 1
- Add the broccoli
- Leave for 2 Min. / counterclockwise / Varoma / Speed 1
- Add water, coconut milk, seasoning, curry, ½ Teaspoon of salt and pepper

- Cook for 10 minutes / counterclockwise / 100°C / Speed 1
- Add sliced carrots
- Cook for 6 minutes more / 100°C / Speed 1

2.8 Cauliflower soup with cream cheese

INGREDIENTS

4 PORTIONS

- 2 onions
- 1 garlic clove
- 1 teaspoon of sunflower oil
- 500g of cauliflower
- 600g of vegetable broth
- 125g of skimmed milk
- Salt and pepper
- 3 tablespoons of cream cheese

PREPARATION

- Introduce the onions and the garlic clove into the mixing bowl
- Chop for 6 seconds / Speed 5
- Push down with the spatula
- Add oil and saute for 3 minutes / 100ºC / Speed 1
- Add the cauliflower, vegetable broth and milk
- Cook for 15 minutes / Varoma / Speed 1
- Add salt, pepper and cream cheese
- Puree during 20 seconds / Speed 8
- Taste and serve

2.9 Mint soup

INGREDIENTS

4 PORTIONS

- 1 onion
- 1 garlic clove
- 500g of diced zucchini
- 100g of potatoes
- 400g of water
- 1 teaspoon of seasoning or 1 broth cube
- 2 teaspoons of freshly chopped mint
- 200g of Feta cheese
- 100g of cooking cream
- 1 tablespoon of olive oil
- 1 pinch of pepper
- 1 pinch of salt

PREPARATION

- Add the onion, garlic and oil into the mixing bowl
- Add butter and saute for 3 minutes / 120ºC / speed 1
- Add the zucchini, potatoes, water, seasoning, a little bit of salt, pepper and the mint   cook for 15 minutes / 100ºC speed 1
- Add the Feta cheese and the cooking cream
- Puree for 50 seconds / speed 6
- Decorate with a mint leaf and a trickle of olive oil

15

2.10 Sweet potato soup

INGREDIENTS

4 PORTIONS

- 500g of sweet potatoes
- 1 piece of ginger
- 0.6L of vegetable broth
- 200g of cream cheese
- 2 tablespoons of aromatic herbs

PREPARATION

- Peel and dice the sweet potatoes and the ginger (size 3x3 cm)
- Add into the mixing bowl
- Add the vegetable broth
- Cook for 20 minutes / 100ºC / speed 2
- Finally, puree for 10 seconds / speed 7
- Add the cream cheese
- Stir for 15 seconds / speed 4
- To end the procedure, add the aromatic herbs
- Stir briefly and serve warm

3. SALADS

3.1 Carrot salad

INGREDIENTS

4 PORTIONS

- 500g of carrot
- 50g of onions cut in halves
- 1 tablespoon of lemon juice
- 3 tablespoons of olive oil
- 1 teaspoon of honey
- 1 teaspoon of salt
- pepper (as desired)

PREPARATION

- Mix all the ingredients in the mixing bowl
- Chop for 6 seconds / speed 5
- Taste and serve at room temperature

3.2 Apple and dates salad

INGREDIENTS

4 PORTIONS

- 100g of orange juice
- ½ lemon
- 150g of yogurt
- 5 apples
- 100g of dates

PREPARATION

- Add the orange juice, half lemon, yogurt and the 5 apples pealed and chop at speed 4
- Remove the seeds from the dates and cut in pieces
- Place the dates under the salad
- Allow it to cool in the fridge for one hour

3.3 Pepper salad

INGREDIENTS

4 PORTIONS

- 50g of almonds
- 2 chilies
- 200g of red pepper
- 200g of yellow pepper
- 1 cucumber
- 30g of olive oil
- 30g of white balsamic
- 1 Teaspoon of salt
- A little quantity of pepper
- 3 Teaspoons of honey (liquid)
- 1 Lemon
- 1 Teaspoon of mustard
- 1 Teaspoon of smoked paprika in powder
- 200g of sheep cheese

PREPARATION

- Chop the chili, parsley and almonds for 4 seconds / speed 8
- Push down with the spatula
- Peel the pepper and remove the seeds. Cut into 4 pieces.

- Slice the cucumber and remove the seeds with a little spoon. Dice the cucumber and put into the mixing bowl.
- Add the oil, balsamic, honey, paprika in powder, salt, pepper and mustard.
- Chop for 5 seconds / speed 4
- Add the sheep cheese and serve in a glass

3.4 Kohlrabi sald

INGREDIENTS

8 PORTIONS

- 500g of diced kohlrabi
- 1 red onion cut in 4 pieces
- 1 apple diced
- 8 dried apricots, small and cut in 4 pieces
- ½ bunch of parsley without stem, chop the leafs
- ½ teaspoon of aromatic herbs
- ¼ teaspoon of freshly ground pepper
- 2 tablespoons of cider vinegar
- 1 tablespoon of olive oil
- 2 trickles of liquid sweetener

PREPARATION

- Add all the ingredients to the mixing bowl
- Chop for 4 seconds / speed 5 help yourself with the spatula

3.5 Broccoli salad

INGREDIENTS

4 PORTIONS

- 300g of broccoli flowers
- 1 piece of red pepper (chopped)
- 1 big apple cut in 4 pieces
- 30g of pinions
- 25g of olive oil
- 15g of apple vinegar
- 1 teaspoon of honey
- 1 teaspoon of mustard
- 1 teaspoon of salt
- ¼ teaspoon of pepper

PREPARATION

- Mix all the ingredients in the mixing bowl
- Chop for 5 seconds / speed 4
- Taste and serve at room temperature

3.6 White cabbage salad

INGREDIENTS

4 PORTIONS

SALAD

- 150g of white cabbage
- 1 carrot
- 1 apple
- ½ red pepper
- Parsley springs

DRESSING

- 1 garlic clove
- 4 parsley springs
- 50ml of sweet cream
- 50g of sour cream
- 50ml of canola oil
- 50ml of cold water
- 1 teaspoon of aromatic herbs
- 25ml of white balsamic
- 1 teaspoon of honey
- 1 teaspoon of mustard
- 1 tablespoon of chopped chives
- 1 tablespoon of chopped herbs

PREPARATION

SALAD

- Wash the white cabbage, peal the carrot, wash the pepper and put away seeds
- Cut the vegetables in big pieces
- Wash the apples, cut into 4 pieces and remove the seeds
- Add everything to the mixing bowl with the parsley
- Chop for 8 seconds / speed 3
- Use the spatula to help yourself
- Set the salad aside

DRESSING

- Peel the garlic cloves
- Put it in the mixing bowl, through the opening of the cover, while working on speed 5
- Wash the parsley and introduce it through the opening and triturate at speed 5
- Add all the other ingredients
- Mix for 10 seconds at speed Turbo to turn it into a sauce
- Add to the salad and mix well

3.7 Carrot and apple salad

INGREDIENTS

4 PORTIONS

- 300g of sliced carrots
- 200g of diced apple
- 15g of sugar
- 15g of lemon juice
- 15g of canola oil

PREPARATION

- Peel the carrot and apples, cut into big pieces
- Add all the ingredients
- Chop for 5 seconds / speed 5
- Push everything down with the spatula
- Chop again for 3 seconds / speed 5
- Ready to be served

3.8 Raw salad

INGREDIENTS

4 PORTIONS

- 5 carrots
- 1 celery
- 1 cucumber
- 1 apple
- 1 Teaspoon of salt

PREPARATION

- Peel the carrot
- Cut the celery and the apple
- Add these ingredients to the Thermomix
- Chop for 30 seconds / speed 8
- Cut the cucumber into small pieces
- Add the cucumber to the previous mix and serve in the mixing bowl
- Add 1 Teaspoon of salt and mix well
- Leave in the fridge for one hour
- Serve

3.9 Bean salad

INGREDIENTS

4 PORTIONS

- 500g of green beans
- 500g of water
- 1 teaspoon of salt
- 1 teaspoon if aromatic herbs for salad
- 1 small onion
- 50g of bacon
- 1 tablespoon of oil
- 1 tablespoon of vinegar
- 1 tablespoon of mustard
- 1 pinch of pepper
- 1 tablespoon of lemon juice
- ½ teaspoon of salt
- Approx. 100 ml of concentrated broth
- 1 pinch of sugar
- 1 teaspoon of lemon and thyme herbs

PREPARATION

- Wash the green beans and cut both ends
- Cut them to an appropriate size and add to the Varoma
- Add 500ml of water with salt and one broth cube
- Cook for 30 minutes / Varoma / speed 1
- Put aside the Varoma and the green beans

- Empty all the liquid
- Add the green beans to the mixing bowl
- Chop the onions in the Thermomix for 5 seconds / speed 5, push ingredients down with help of the spatula
- Add the bacon
- Add an oil jet (approximately 2 Tablespoons)
- Cook for 4 minutes / Varoma / speed 1/ counterclockwise
- Add broth, remaining oil and all the aromatic herbs
- Stir for 5 seconds / speed 1
- Add to the warm green beans
- Allow it to settle for 2 hours

3.10 Papaya salad

INGREDIENTS / 6 PORTIONS

DRESSING

- 2 red peppers
- 2 garlic cloves
- 2 tablespoons of soy sauce
- 2 tablespoons of fish sauce
- 1 teaspoon of brown sugar
- 2 tablespoons of lime juice
- 1 tablespoon of anchovy sauce (optional)

VEGETABLES

- 2 Tablespoons of toasted peanuts, preferably without salt
- 200g of green papaya / carrot, or both
- 2 metro green beans
- 8 Cherry tomatoes

PREPARATION

- Chop the peanuts for 2 seconds / speed 5
- Empty
- Chop the pepper and the garlic for 3 seconds / speed 7
- Add the other ingredients of the dressing and mix for 5 seconds / speed 5
- Empty

- Add the papaya and the carrot into the mixing bowl
- Chop for 3 seconds / speed 5
- Cut the Cherry tomatoes in half, cut the beans in 2 cm long pieces
- Mix all the ingredients well, except for the peanuts and serve on a tray
- Spray with the peanuts and serve.

4. MAIN COURSES

4.1 Potato and cauliflower stew

INGREDIENTS

4 PORTIONS

- 1 small cauliflower cut in big pieces
- 1 chopped onion
- 1 tablespoon of oil
- 5 medium potatoes, cut in small dices
- 1 can of crushed tomatoes 400g
- 1 teaspoon of ground cumin seeds
- 1 teaspoon of crushed coriander seeds
- 1 teaspoon de turmeric powder
- 1 teaspoon of curry powder
- 1 teaspoon of garam Masalta
- 1 teaspoon of salt
- 2 teaspoons of seasoning or one vegetable broth cube
- 1 bunch of coriander chopped stems and crushed leaves, prepare it separately and in advanced!

PREPARATION

- Add the cauliflower to the mixing bowl
- Chop for 3 seconds / speed 3
- Add oil into the mixing bowl

- Add the onions
- Cook for 2 minutes / counterclockwise / speed Varoma
- Add herbs (except basic vegetables)
- Cook for 3 more minutes / speed Varoma
- Add tomatoes and cook for 3 minutes / 100°C / counterclockwise
- Put the basket as a cover to avoid splashing
- Add the diced potatoes
- At the end add the basic vegetables
- When all potatoes are in the mixing bowl, cook for 15 minutes / 100°C / counterclockwise, add the basket as a cover to avoid splashing
- Add chopped cauliflower and the chopped coriander bunch
- Cook for 15 Min. / 100°C / counterclockwise
- Finally, add chopped coriander leaves, taste and serve.

4.2 Tomato and arugula risotto

INGREDIENTS

4 PORTIONS

- 80g of parmesan cheese
- 1 sprig of rosemary
- 4 tablespoons of olive oil
- 120g of shallots
- 2 garlic cloves
- 60g of dried tomato
- 320g of risotto
- 600g of peeled and diced tomatoes
- 0.1 liter of white wine
- 0.6 liters of hot vegetable broth
- 1 tablespoon of tomato paste
- 50g of pine nuts
- 1 bunch of arugula
- 1 pinch of salt, sugar and pepper
- 100g of black boneless olives
- 3 tablespoons of fresh cream (Crème fraîche)
- 1 pinch of Cayenne

PREPARATION

- Add the parmesan cheese and the rosemary branch into the mixing bowl

- Chop for 10 seconds / speed 10, empty and wash the bowl
- Chop the dried tomato, shallots and garlic cloves for 5 seconds / speed 6
- Push ingredients down with help of the spatula, add the tomato paste
- Add the olives and the olive oil, cook for 3 minutes / Varoma / speed 1
- Add the risotto, cook for 3 minutes / speed 1 / 100ºC
- Add salt, pepper, cayenne and sugar
- Cool down with white wine, heat for 1 minute / 100ºC / speed 1
- Add the warm vegetable broth
- Stir the rice with the spatula in order to prevent it from sticking
- Cook for approx. 20 minutes / 90ºC / speed 1
- Remove the measuring cup; add the basket as a cover of the mixing bowl
- Meanwhile, toast the pine nuts in a pan till they get a golden color
- Wash the arugula
- 1 minute before you finish cooking, add the tomato dices, the fresh cream and the mixture of Parmesan cheese and rosemary
- Add salt and pepper
- Stir for 12 seconds /counterclockwise / speed 4 and let rest shortly
- Taste and cover, allow to settle for 2 minutes
- Before serving, spray with pine nuts and arugula

4.3 Beans stew

INGREDIENTS

4 PORTIONS

- 200g of diced carrot
- 200g of chopped celery
- 30g of sliced butter
- 500g of potatoes cut in small pieces
- 500g of green beans, frozen, thawed or fresh, cut in halves
- 600g of water
- 1 broth cube
- 1 dried savory
- ½ teaspoon of salt
- ½ teaspoon of pepper

PREPARATION

- Add carrot and celery to the mixing bowl

- Chop for 5 seconds / speed 5

- Push ingredients down with help of the spatula

- Add butter

- Strain for 3 minutes / 120ºC / Varoma / counterclockwise / speed 1

- Add the potatoes, beans, water, broth cube, savory, salt and pepper

- Cook for 18 minutes / 100ºC / speed 1
- Taste and serve

4.4 Chicken, vegetables and rice stew

INGREDIENTS

4 PERSON

- 500g of chicken breast, cut in small pieces
- 1 onion
- 2 garlic cloves
- 1 tablespoon of butter
- 200g of rice
- 1L of water
- 1 teaspoon of vegetal paste
- vegetables:
- 1 red and 1 yellow pepper cut in stripes
- 1 sliced carrot
- 1 sliced zucchini
- Some corn and dried beans

SAUCE

- 250g of broth
- 100g of white wine
- 20g of starch
- salt
- pepper
- Nutmeg
- Cayenne

PREPARATION

- Add the meat, salt and pepper into the Varoma
- Add the vegetables and salt slightly
- Add onion and garlic cloves into the mixing bowl
- Chop for 5 seconds / speed 5
- Add butter
- Cook for 5 minutes / Varoma / speed 1
- Add water and vegetable paste
- Attach hook and weigh rice
- Cover Varoma and allow to cook for 25 minutes / Varoma / speed 1
- Remove Varoma and basket, keep warm
- Allow it to absorb the liquid and add the ingredients for the sauce
- Mix for 5 seconds / speed 5
- Cook for 5 minutes / 100ºC / speed 2

4.5 Curry and vegetables rice

INGREDIENTS

4 PORTIONS

- 200g of rice
- 700g of fresh vegetables, such as carrot, cauliflower, beans, broccoli, green peas, zucchini
- 1L of water
- 150g of cashew seeds
- 1 tablespoon of canola oil
- 1 chopped garlic clove
- 1 teaspoon of powder chili
- 1 can of coconut milk (400ml)
- 1 tablespoon of powder vegetable broth
- 1 teaspoon of powder curry
- 4-8 tablespoons of soy sauce

PREPARATION

- Weigh rice in basket
- Add water into the Thermomix and introduce rice, cover, add Varoma
- Chop vegetables into small pieces
- Add the vegetables to the Varoma, cover
- Cook for 25 minutes / Varoma / speed 1
- Toast the cashew seeds in a pan
- Empty the cashew seeds

- Warm up the canola oil in the pan
- Add the garlic cloves and one Teaspoon of powder chili
- Add the coconut milk as it cool down
- Add vegetable broth in powder, curry powder and soy sauce. Let it boil shortly
- Add vegetables and cashew to the sauce, mix and serve
- Serve with rice

4.6 Vegetable stuffed peppers

INGREDIENTS

5 PORTIONS

- 5 peppers
- 200g of dry millet
- 1 vegetable broth cube
- 0.8 liters of water
- 1 pack of butter with vegetables, approx. 300g
- 1 can of grilled vegetables

PREPARATION

- Boil water with the broth cube
- Add the dry millet
- Boil at low temperature till the whole water has been absorbed
- Add the butter to the millet
- Mix the coconut milk with the canned vegetables
- Mix the sauce with the vegetables and the millet
- Wash the peppers
- Cut the "top" of the peppers and reserve
- Cleanse seeds and stem
- Fill generously the peppers with the vegetable and millet mix
- Once full, put the "top" back to the pepper
- Fix with a toothpick

- Fill the Thermomix with approx. 1 liter of water
- Add the stuffed peppers to the Varona and close
- Add the Varoma in the Thermomix
- Cook the peppers for 30 minutes / Varoma / speed 1

4.7 Squids

INGREDIENTS

4 PORTIONS

- 800g of squid (cut into rings without breading)
- 300g of crushed tomatoes
- 250g of green peas
- 15g of dried mushrooms
- 4 anchovies
- 2 garlic cloves
- 1 bunch of parsley
- 1 pinch of grounded chilies
- 100ml of white wine, dry
- 20ml of olive oil
- ½ teaspoon of salt
- 1 vegetable broth cube
- 1 pinch of pepper

PREPARATION

- Add the garlic cloves and the parsley to the mixing bowl
- Chop for 3 seconds / speed 5
- Add the olive oil, the grounded chilies and anchovies
- Sauté for 3 minutes / 100ºC / speed 1
- Add the dried mushrooms through the opening of the lid, also add the White wine and the squid

- Cook for 5 minutes / 100ºC / counterclockwise
- Add the crushed tomato, salt, pepper and broth cube
- Cook for 25 minutes / 100ªC / speed 3 / counterclockwise
- Serve the squid with its sauce accompanied by some rice

4.8 Noodles wth salmon

INGREDIENTS

2 PORTIONS

MAIN COURSE

- 2 salmon fillets / thawed
- 750g of water
- 200g of noodles
- Salt

SAUCE

- 100g of broth
- 100g of cooking cream
- 100g of milk
- 15g of flour
- 1 teaspoon of vegetable powder seasoning
- 1 tablespoon of aromatic herbs
- White pepper

PREPARATION

MAIN COURSE

- Introduce the salmon fillets into the Varoma
- Add the water and salt into the Thermomix
- Introduce the Varoma and cook for 15 minutes / Varoma / speed 1

- Put Varoma aside and weight the noodles
- Cook for 10 minutes / Varoma / speed 1
- Put the Varoma aside
- Remove the noodles and drain the liquid

SAUCE

- Add all the ingredients into the Thermomix
- Cook for 4 minutes / 100ºC / speed 4
- Serve in 2 plates and enjoy

4.9 Salmon fillet with potatoes and broccoli

INGREDIENTS

4 PORTIONS

- 500g of broccoli
- 500g of water
- 1 vegetable broth cube
- 800g of potatoes
- 1 lemon
- 600g of salmon fillet without skin
- ½ teaspoon of salt
- ¼ teaspoon of pepper
- 1 bunch of fresh dill
- 100g of cooking cream

PREPARATION

- Add the broccoli to the Varoma
- Add water and the broth cube to the Thermomix
- Insert the basket and weight the potatoes
- Add the Varoma
- Cook for 12 minutes / Varoma / speed 1
- Squeeze the lemon
- Place the salmon in the Varoma with some salt, pepper, lemon, and one branch of fresh dill

- After a short previous cooking, carefully place the base of the Varoma
- Cook for 14 minutes / Varoma / speed 1
- Place Varoma aside, place basket aside, empty the Thermomix and save the liquid
- Add 300g of the liquid, 100g of potatoes, the cooking cream and the rest of the dill to the Thermomix
- Puree progressively during 30 seconds / speed 4-6-8
- Taste and add salt, pepper and lemon juice to taste
- Serve the fish with vegetables and potatoes

4.10 Cauliflower and zucchini pancakes

INGREDIENTS

4 PORTIONS

- 350g of cauliflower / approx. ½ cauliflower
- 250g of zucchini
- 1 teaspoon of salt
- 1 teaspoon of curry
- 1 pinch of pepper
- 2 eggs
- 4 tablespoons of flour
- Oil

PREPARATION

- Dice the cauliflower and the zucchini
- Add to the Thermomix
- Add salt, pepper and curry
- Chop for 6 seconds / speed 4
- Add the eggs and flour
- Mix counterclockwise during 12 seconds / speed 4
- Oil the pan
- Add Tablespoon size heaps of the Thermomix mixture into the pan
- Rotate when golden
- Finish cooking and serve

5. DESSERTS

5.1 Pear mousse with chia seeds

INGREDIENTS

2 PORTIONS

- 2 mature pears
- 5 teaspoons of chia seeds
- 200g of soy yogurt
- 4-5 tablespoons of agave Syrup
- 1 tablespoon of mixed nuts
- 1-4 leaves of basil

PREPARATION

- Peel the pears and remove seeds
- Introduce the pears and a Tablespoon of Agave Syrup into the mixing bowl
- Puree for 30 seconds / speed 6
- Add the yogurt, the rest of the agave syrup and the chia seeds
- Mix for 15 seconds / speed 2
- Let it settle for 20 minutes
- Pour in a glass layer by layer
- Garnish with basil leaves and nuts

5.2 Fruit ice cream

INGREDIENTS

8 PORTIONS

- 400g of frozen fruit, for example raspberries or strawberries
- 2 egg whites (fresh)
- 100g of milk
- 2 tablespoons of liquid sweetener

PREPARATION

- Add fruit to mixing bowl
- Chop for 20 seconds / speed 10
- Add egg whites, milk and liquid sweetener
- Stir for 10 seconds / speed 6
- Move the Ingredients to one side with the help of the spatula to be able to connect the mixer
- Place the mixer
- Mix for 2 minutes / speed until creamy
- Serve immediately

5.3 Banana ice cream with basil

INGREDIENTS

4 PORTIONS

- 300g of mature frozen banana
- 10 fresh basil leaves
- ½ lemon zest
- 1 ripe banana (in pieces)

PREPARATION

- Add frozen banana in chunks, basil leaves and lemon zest in the mixing bowl
- Chop for 10 seconds / speed 10
- Add the ripe banana
- Mix for 5 seconds / speed 6
- Serve immediately

5.4 Ginger tea

INGREDIENTS

1 LITER

- Approx. 20g of ginger
- 1.5 liter of water
- ½ lemon squeezed
- 30g of agave syrup

PREPARATION

- Add the ginger to the mixing bowl
- Chop for 6 seconds / speed 8
- Add 1.5 liters of water
- Stir during 13 minutes / 80ºC / speed 1
- Add the squeezed lemon and the agave syrup
- Stir for 10 seconds / speed 2
- Pour the ginger tea through a strainer into a teapot

5.5 Strawberry milkshake

INGREDIENTS

2 PORTIONS

- 150g of frozen strawberries
- 600g of cold milk
- 1 trickle of liquid sweetener

PREPARATION

- Add frozen strawberries into the mixing bowl
- Chop for 30 seconds / speed 10
- Push Ingredients down with the help of spatula
- Add cold milk and liquid sweetener
- Mix for 20 seconds / speed 10

5.6 Yogurt ice cream with strawberry sauce

INGREDIENTS

2 PORTIONS

YOGURT ICE CREAM

- 250g of natural yogurt
- 1 tablespoon of sugared vanilla
- 1 teaspoon of honey

STRAWBERRY SAUCE

- 100g of strawberries, natural, frozen or thawed
- 1 teaspoon of vanilla sugar
- 1 teaspoon of lemon juice

PREPARATION

YOGURT ICE CREAM

- Add the ingredients for the ice cream in the mixing bowl
- Stir to make creamy for 5 minutes / speed 4
- Introduce the yogurt into the ice cream maker for 30 minutes
- If you do not have an ice cream maker: Put the yogurt in a freezer bag and put it in the freezer for 30 minutes,

knead it once and put it back into the freezer. After 3 hours it will be ready.

STRAWBERY SAUCE

-   Puree the strawberries with sugared vanilla and lemon juice for 30 seconds / speed 8
-   Pour in a glass one layer of frozen yogurt and one layer of sauce and so on till full
-   Decorate with fresh fruit or chocolate shavings

5.7 Lemon tea with ginger

INGREDIENTS

8 GLASSES

- 100g of peeled ginger
- 3 lemons
- 100g of honey
- 15 mint leaves

PREPARATION

- Peel the ginger and cut into pieces
- Fill mixing bowl with 100g of water
- Heat during 3 minutes / 100ºC / speed 1
- Chop the ginger for 10 seconds / speed 8
- Add the remaining 900g of water
- Cook for 6 minutes / 100ºC
- Let it settle for 20 minutes
- Go through the strainer
- Add the lemon juice and sweeten it with acacia honey

5.8 Orange and pineapple smoothie

INGREDIENTS

2 PORTIONS

- 150g of oranges
- 150g of pineapple
- 1 teaspoon of vanilla sugar

PREPARATION

- Peel the oranges and pineapple
- Remove possible seeds
- Cut into big pieces and insert in the Thermomix
- Add sugar vanilla
- Puree for 30 seconds / speed 10 and enjoy directly

5.9 Raspberry ice cream

3 PORTIONS

- 300g of ultra-frozen raspberries without added sugars
- 200g of cottage cheese

PREPARATION

- Add ultra-frozen raspberries and cottage cheese in the mixing bowl
- Mix all ingredients for 20 seconds / speed 6

5.10 Fruit salad with raspberry yogurt

INGREDIENTS

4 PORTIONS

FRUIT SALAD

- 1 apple
- 1 pear
- The juice from 1 orange
- 1 banana

RASPBERRY YOGURT

- 125g of raspberries
- 375g of yogurt
- 2 teaspoons of vanilla sugar

PREPARATION

FRUIT SALAD

- Cut 4 apples and pears
- Add the juice of an orange in the mixing bowls
- Chop for 3 seconds / speed 4
- Add the banana
- Chop for 2 seconds / speed 4
- Empty the content in a separate bowl
- Clean and dry the mixing bowl

RASPBERRY YOGURT

- Add the raspberries to the mixing bowl
- Chop for 10 seconds / speed 8
- Add the yogurt and sugar vanilla
- Stir for 30 seconds / speed 4
- Serve raspberry yogurt over fruit salad

6. APPETIZERS, DIPPING SAUCES AND SPREADS

6.1 Tomato and cottage cheese dipping sauce

INGREDIENTS

2 PORTIONS

- ½ onion
- ½ teaspoon of salt
- ½ teaspoon of pepper
- 1 teaspoon de olive oil
- 7 dried tomatoes
- 2 garlic cloves
- 1 glass of cottage cheese
- 1 mixing tablespoon of herbs with salt

PREPARATION

- Put the onion, garlic cloves and dried tomatoes in the Thermomix
- Grind for 7 seconds / speed 8
- Push down with the spatula
- Add cottage cheese, salt, pepper and herbs in the Thermomix
- Mix for 20 seconds / speed 5

6.2 Spreading avocado and dates cream

INGREDIENTS

1 GLASS

- 2 dates (boneless)
- 1 avocado
- ½ persimmon
- 1 teaspoon of curry
- ½ teaspoon of herbal salt

PREPARATION

- Chop the dates for 8 seconds / speed 8
- Add all the remaining Ingredients
- Stir for 10 seconds / speed 5

6.3 Spreading salmon cream

INGREDIENTS

4 PERSON

- 1 onion, cut in 4 pieces
- 200g of smoked salmon
- 3 hard-boiled eggs, halved
- 200g of cream cheese

PREPARATION

- Chop the onion for 3 seconds / speed 5
- Add the other ingredients and stir during 5 seconds / speed 5

6.4 Dates dipping sauce

INGREDIENTS

1 PORTION

- 150g of dates, dried and boneless
- 250g of white beans, (canned, drained)
- 1 garlic clove
- 100g of soy natural yogurt
- 50g of soy cream
- 50g of vegan spreads
- 1 tablespoon of lemon juice
- 2 teaspoons of curry
- 1 teaspoon of paprika
- ½ teaspoon of salt
- 1 teaspoon of chili, according to taste

PREPARATION

- Add the beans, dates and garlic to the mixing bowl
- Chop for 10 seconds / speed 8
- Add the remaining ingredients
- Stir for 20 seconds / speed 6
- Taste, add salt and chili to taste

6.5 Persimmon jam

INGREDIENTS

5 PORTIONS

- 750g of persimmons, skinned and cut into dice
- 250g apple, washed, skinned, and all seeds removed
- 1 lemon, washed and grated the peel
- 500g of 2:1 gelatinizing sugar
- 20g ginger

PREPARATION

- Chop ginger and lemon peel for 5 seconds / speed 8 / counterclockwise and with lid closed
- Add pieces of persimmon and apple. Chop for 5 seconds / speed 8 / counterclockwise
- Stir the half-lemon juice and the gelatinizing sugar briefly (normal direction)
- Cook for 13 minutes / 100°C / speed 2 / counterclockwise
- Fill with glasses rinsed with hot water and allow it to cool

6.6 Eggplant pesto

INGREDIENTS

2 GLASSES

FOR THE FIRST STEP

- 80g of eggplant
- 60g of red pepper
- 1 big garlic clove
- 40g of olive oil

FOR THE SECOND STEP

- 40g of dried tomato in oil
- 70g of tomato paste

FOR THE LAST STEP

- 20g of pine nuts (toasted to the pan)
- 20g of Pecorino (grated)
- 5g of basil (a handful)
- A pinch of salt
- Freshly ground pepper
- A pinch of sugar
- Chili
- 30g of olive oil

PREPARATION

FIRST STEP

- Wash the vegetables and chop
- Add all contents to the mixing bowl
- Chop for 3 seconds / speed 5
- Cook for 10 minutes / speed 1 / Varoma (without measuring vessel)

SECOND STEP

- Cut the tomatoes into thin pieces
- Add it to the other ingredients of the bowl
- Cook for 5 minutes / speed 2 / Varoma uncovered

LAST STEP

- Add all remaining ingredients
- Mix for 10 seconds / speed 6
- Add the pesto in glasses and cover with a little olive oil

6.7 Yogurt appetizer with fruit and muesli

INGREDIENTS

6 PORTIONS

FRUIT LAYER

- 500g of varied fruit, for example 2 apples, 2 bananas, 100g of strawberries, and 100g of melon

YOGURT LAYER

- 650g of yogurt
- 50g milk

CRUSTY LAYER

- 1 pack of muesli or chocolate flakes

PREPARATION

FRUIT LAYER

- Chop the fruit (previously peeled and seeded) and introduce in the Thermomix
- Chop for 2 seconds / speed 5
- Empty and store aside

YOGURT LAYER

- Add yogurt, sugar and milk to the Thermomix
- Stir for 15 seconds / speed 4

STACK LAYERS

- In 6 glasses, first put the layer of yogurt, carefully put the layer of fruit, and finally the crusty layer
- Repeat until all ingredients are finished
- To finish, put a crusty layer of fruit in the center to decorate

6.8 Spreading bean cream

INGREDIENTS

1 GLASS

- 1 onion
- 10g of oil
- 1 can of beans (255g drained weight), drained and washed
- 1 teaspoon of marjoram
- 1 trickle of lemon juice
- 1 teaspoon of parsley
- Salt and pepper
- 1 teaspoon of chives

PREPARATION

- Chop the onions for 3 seconds / speed 5
- Add the oil and steeping during 3 minutes / speed 2 / 100ºC
- Add the rest of Ingredients
- Puree for 10 seconds / speed 5

6.9 Dates and sesame spreading cream

INGREDIENTS

1 GLASS

- 200g of seedless dates
- 100g of water
- 150g of sesame paste

PREPARATION

- Add water and the dates to the Thermomix
- Set it to 3 minutes / Varoma / speed 3
- Add sesame paste, set to 5 seconds / speed 10
- Fill glasses rinsed with hot water with cream and let it cool
- Once cooled, store in a refrigerator

6.10 Turkish style spreading cream

INGREDIENTS

1 PORTIONS

- 1 garlic clove
- 1 bunch of parsley
- 100g of cream cheese
- 100g of fresh cheese
- 3 teaspoons of de Ajvar
- 1 pinch of salt
- 1 pinch of pepper

PREPARATION

- Add the parsley and garlic clove to the Thermomix
- Chop for 5 seconds / speed 4
- Add the cream cheese, fresh cheese, Ajvar, salt and pepper
- Mix for 25 seconds / speed 3

Printed in Great Britain
by Amazon